Everlasting Love Poems

Dr. Rhemalyn Lewis-Williams

Meredith
a small press

Etc

Blog: meredithetc.com

facebook **Meredith Etc**

🐦 **Meredithetc**

A Meredith *Etc* Book

Meredith *Etc*
1052 Maria Court
Jackson, Mississippi 39204-5151
www.meredithetc.com

Keywords: acrostic poems, love poems, relationships, couples, inspirational poems

Published simultaneously by Meredith *Etc*
in softcover/hardback
Trade paperback 6"x 9" printed by CreateSpace
ISBN-13: 978-0692624326
ISBN-10: 0692624325
Black & White on White paper
52 pages

Available on the World Wide Web as an eBook
Printed and bound in the United States of America

First Printing
Hardback Edition
Printed by Nook Press
Black & White on Cream paper

Visit Dr. Rhemalyn Lewis-Williams author page online.
http://meredithetc.com/everlasting-love-poems/

DEDICATION

I dedicate **_Everlasting Love Poems_** to my immediate family: husband, Sam, son, Keterrious, daughters Kenecia and Diamond, and grandson, Caiden, and to the bonding bliss and solidarity of couples around the world.

ACKNOWLEDGMENTS

I acknowledge the support of several important individuals in my life whose guidance, support, and encouragement made the completion of this book possible. First and foremost, I acknowledge the Spirit of the Lord. Thank you Father! Secondly, I recognize my precious husband, Sam (my number 1 fan) and children Keterrious, Kenecia, and Diamond for being there, believing, looking up to your mother, and caring for me.

I also appreciate my siblings, especially Brenda, Lauritta; to my brother Duron K. Lewis who contributed chapter illustrations; to my dear nieces, particularly Ajasiz, Makeba, Angela and Amelia, who are also my friends; to my friend, Dr. Marjuyua Lartey, who is like a sister; to my cousins Vita, Dorothy, and Kerensa; and my relatives and church family. I love you all and thanks for everything.

Everlasting Love Poems

CONTENTS

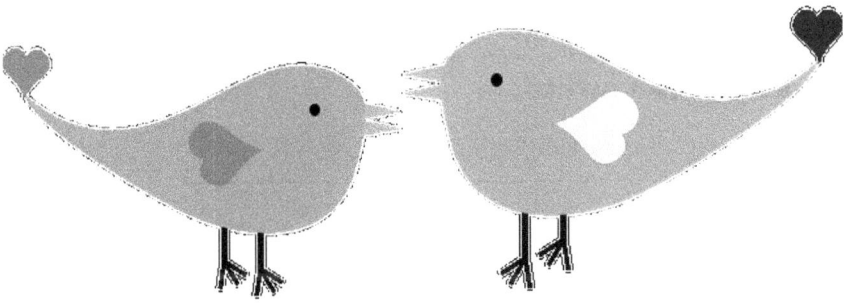

Love is kind, patient, pleasing, exciting...

This book is a gift to:

_____

From _____

DATE _____

PREFACE

I wrote 52 acrostic poems that provide a framework for positive communication, a critical part of reinvigorating relationships, which is significant because positive and uplifting words stimulate love and strengthens couple bonding.

For those of you who may not know, acrostic poems use the first letter in a word to spell out a word, phrase, or sentence which may or may not rhyme. Like other forms of poetry, they tell a story. I used my first name "Rhemalyn" to create the following acrostic poem:

Rhemalyn is my name.
Heaven is my aim.
Enchanting I shall be,
Moving toward perfection, can't you see?
Advantageous, like my father,
Living single wasn't a bother.
You can be as successful, too!
Nonetheless, I'm no different from you.

The beginning.

On November 2, 2014, a "voice" in a dream told me to write 12 acrostic poems about relationships. I ignored the "voice;" then, I dreamed the same dream two more times. The third dream confirmed that I must obey HIS voice.

Shortly afterward, I contacted a sorority sister, Ty A. Patterson, Author/Poet, *Southern Jewel: The Elements Within*, and told her about my dreams and expressed how I didn't understand why the "voice" emphasized the number 12. Ty suggested I write a poem for the 12 calendar months; immediately, I was flabbergasted! After receiving consultation from my publisher, I was informed I needed more than 12 poems for a book of poetry; therefore, I decided to create 52 for the weeks in a calendar year.

Dear hearts, whether you are single, married, female, or male, it is my belief that this collection of poems will enhance the spread of optimistic ideas, and embolden the lives of lovable beings.

Enjoy *Everlasting Love Poems* and tell others about it so it can trickle one reader at a time through the world of literature.

Advance Praise for **_Everlasting Love Poems_**

Everlasting Love Poems teases us with wordplay on the many attributes of love and relationships. This book takes us from the first glance at a love interest to the ins and outs of being in love. I enjoyed every poem in this book and believe it will touch your heart and enlighten your love journey.

Marjuyua Lartey-Rowser, PhD,
Hattiesburg, MS

Everlasting Love Poems is a must read, especially for those who want to begin a riveting journey exploring one of the most discussed, yet most nebulous subjects, _love._

Albert W. Carter, PhD
Jackson, MS

This is a collection of poems that can easily be digested and acted upon by ANY couple, or those seeking to have a healthy relationship. Not only did the poet create eye catching words, she told stories that touched on the HOW TO part of love.

Poet Ty A. Patterson

Southern Jewel: The Elements Within
Jackson, MS

Everlasting Love Poems can serve as a guide to any relationship (new and old)! These poems are truthful, uplifting, and inspiring. I read each poem with great enthusiasm, but I think my favorite is "Ardent"! A definite must read!

Ajasiz Johnson, MA, Author
ABCs, 123s, Help Me, Please!
Memphis, TN

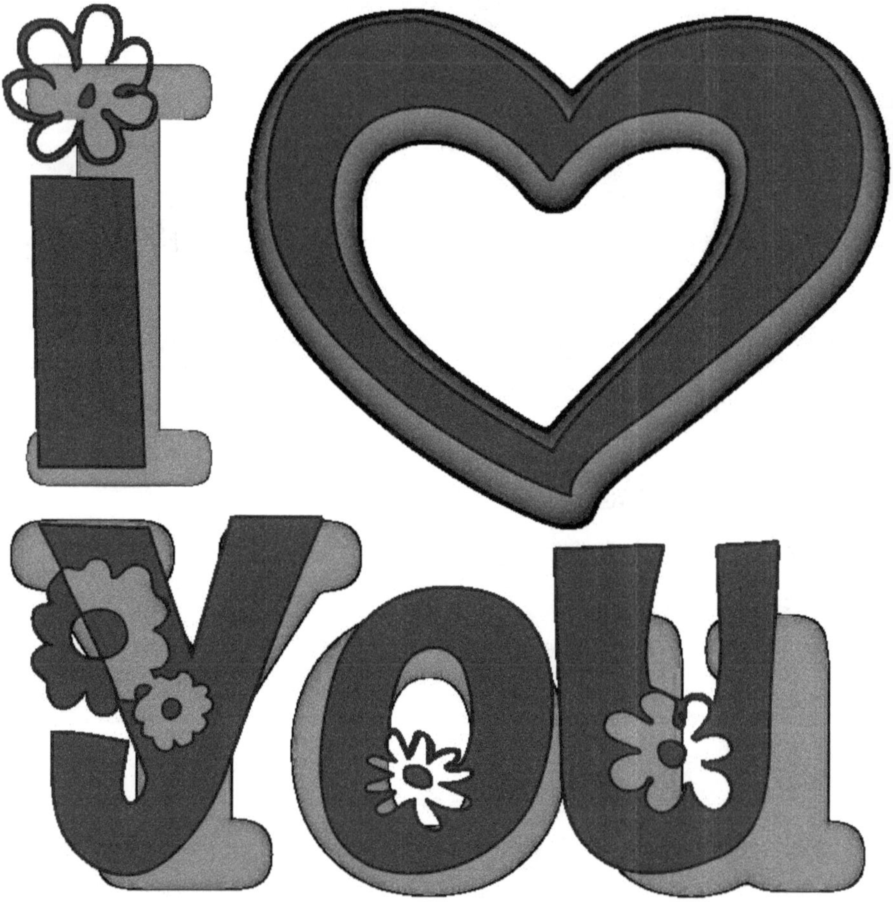
I
YOU

ONE

Passion

Chapter One - Passion

Passion is defined as "love chemicals" which join two things or people together with expectancy or a fiery desire, and as the state of a person feeling strong love or sexual desire toward someone.

Poem List:

1. Romeo
2. Juliet
3. Inamorato
4. Inamorata
5. Understanding
6. Ardent
7. Intimacy
8. Zeal
9. Symmetry
10. Alliance
11. Aptness
12. Homogeneity
13. Tranquil

1. ROMEO

Recognizing the love that was shown by him
Only solidifies the
Magnitude of how you should
Establish your relationship
On a continuous basis.

2. Juliet

Just as he had shown his love, she revealed her
Undying affection by
Letting go of all negative surroundings because
It will certainly
Explain what
True love is all about even after death.

3. Inamorato

I promise to love you more while
Never leaving you confused because I
Am
Mesmerized by your
Obvious beautiful appearance
Realizing that you
Are my soul mate, I can
Tell you no lie, we are
Opposite, that's why we attract.

4. Inamorata

I promise to love you forever and
Never let you go
Astray because you
Mean so much to me
On the other side of the
Rainbow will you get the
Answer
To the problem of
A woman that loves so much.

5. Understanding

Uniquely selecting the more perfect mate through
prayer while asking God for revelation
Never fails when you are trying to
Decipher what is being said and who is being sent
Enables you to empower yourself through
Relentless comprehension, but
Sometimes there may be differences in opinions;
That is when each of you should
Analyze yourselves and
Never forget the
Detriment that may have arisen
In your relationship from the gap of
Not attempting to
Gain more solutions to the problem than the issue.

6. Ardent

Always answer without arguing.
Respond in a positive manner.
Doll him or her with grave passion.
Entertain each other's presence.
Notwithstanding any adverse attitudes, always
Trust and believe in each other without wavering.

7. Intimacy

In times of sadness, both mates can amazingly show the
Need for one another as well as be
Thoughtful and considerate toward each other's
Inner feelings; this is done by two very
Mature adults who
Altruistically have undying love and is
Candid about feelings toward each other,
Yet set for an eternity filled with everlasting love.

8. Zeal

Zoning into the other person's arms makes an
Everlasting revelation that will
Always
Leave a strong impression.

9. Symmetry

Since both of you are halves that once said,
Yes!
Many are happy for your
Memories of
Enchanting partnership that is a
Tenacious
Revelation that
Yields a successful ending.

10. Alliance

Altogether you will become one
Loving soul matched with
Laughter. It will
Increase your
Aptitude of greatness to
Nearly a thousand fold with
Charismatic comfort and
Energetic love.

11. Aptness

As you struggle from day-to-day
Physically you are
Tied together tactfully to
Never fall apart as you
Enter into a very
Savvy
Sensitive relationship.

11. Homogeneity

Humbleness is a great attribute
Of any relationship or
Marriage that
Often times
Generate a likeness for
Each other due to an important
Nature as an
Equal, elegant and
Intriguing
Tale of people together who
Yearn for each other's love.

12. Tranquil

Through any turbulent time
Relax and unwind.
Ask yourself this question,
Need I another mate?
Question 2, Am I on a date?
Unforgettably you should leave an impression.
If you are truly
Living to learn a lesson.

TWO
Affection

Chapter Two – Affection

Affection relates to "love, passion, and closeness." **Affection** reveals a kind feeling of love which is a zealous, tender attachment of emotion or love.

Poem List:

1. Hug
2. Care
3. Love
4. Warm
5. Bond
6. Joy
7. Charm
8. Enchant
9. Fond
10. Gregarious
11. Effervescent
12. Affinity
13. Inspire

1. Hug

Having someone that is there for you
Under any circumstance, will always
Give one a sense of self-worth.

2. Care

Care and concern for each other
Are essential ingredients to a healthy
Relationship that will result in
Everlasting love.

3. Love

Living with your soul mate on any given night is worth
more than being alone
On a sunny morning. When you have found that
compatibility you will be
Very happy to know that he or she will
Ensure their love forever.

4. Warm

When being with your "boo"
Always say what's true
Revealing a lie will
Make him or her fly.

5. Bond

Being with that "special" someone is a blessing
and has an
Oomph that can
Never be
Destroyed.

6. Joy

Just as you have met
On a sunny day
Your smile keeps me forever.

7. Charm

Cheering each other on is not a
Hard thing to do.
Always listen and
Respond with a
Meaningful solution.

8. Enchant

Entering a delightful friendship
Never lets you go astray.
Cleverly treat each other more than
Half of 200% because you are so
Alluring with attractive
Needs. Believing in each other
Tells how much you care.

9. Fond

Feeling special to
Others attention is
Noteworthy achievements that
Deserve receptiveness.

10. Gregarious

Gathering together socially with
Realness at its best while
Entertaining each other's presence
Goes equal in an
Advantageous manner that will be
Refreshing as a fragrance, and
Instilling as peace. Your
Original thoughts won't be
Uneven as you
Swing into his or her arms.

11. Effervescent

Exciting and vivacious that you are
Freely and
Fun-loving thus far. As we
Embark upon and
Reflect, we are always
Victorious!
Each of our souls are
Similar because we are
Caring individuals that
Enjoy
Never ending
Tenacious love.

12. Affinity

A feeling of closeness that one happens to
Fulfill your needs with, will
Forever create
Inventions of
Nobel,
Interactions,
Toward
You.

13. Inspire

In all that is required, encouragement is
Needed to
Secure each other's feelings, so is being
Patient to help
Increase
Relevance in
Every moment spent.

THREE

Connection

Chapter Three – Connection

Connection is like "two peas in a pod" working together harmoniously. Connection is defined as the act of bringing two things into contact, especially communication.

Poem List:

1. Spiritual
2. Commitment
3. Devote
4. Adore
5. Avuncular
6. Loyalty
7. Trust
8. Share
9. Enjoy
10. Monotony
11. Harmony
12. Godspeed
13. Apposite

1. Spiritual

Submitting yourselves to the "Most High" is
Perpetually the wisest thing to do.
In that blessings will be
Reaped,
In all shapes, forms and fashions.
Then, there's a completeness with
Understanding to
Always
Linger.

2. Commitment

Coming together as one, clearly validates each
Others' promise to devote undying assurance that
Maintains stability in a relationship. Seeking good
Mannerism is always a plus to help strengthen the
Insecurities of an individual who
Tend to doubt, but together you two can
Mesmerize each other while celebrating the
Enjoyment of a
Never ending love story
That doesn't fade away.

3. Devote

Desiring that special someone is so
Endearing, and shows a
Vivid imagination
Of what it would be like not
To have them for
Eternity.

4. Adore

As you say that you are
Devoted to each
Other, the unwavering faithfulness
Refreshes your
Every thought.

5. Avuncular

As with your aunt and uncle's love that shows
Very similar feelings will be
Unleashed with seemingly
Nice and indulging
Care that remains
Upbeat with
Long lasting
And
Realistic love.

6. Loyalty

Living a lie will not set you free from the
Opposition that
You will receive from your significant other.
After a thing called, "infidelity" is introduced; neither
is
Luck because it
Teaches us evil and
Yields a breakdown of despair.

7. Trust

Thinking back to the very first time you met, the
Realization sets in that often intertwines with
Unity to give each other a more,
Surmountable beginning and end
That will last forever.

12. Share

Sensitive to your mates every need, want, desire and
feelings are one thing.
However, there's more to it; you should
Always come together solely when you
Realize that your bond will last through
Eternity.

13. Enjoy

Encamped in his or her arms,
Never makes one sad; you will become
Jollied with joy and receive,
Outstanding happiness
Youthfully together.

14. Monotony

Meeting at a simultaneous point while
Obliging a
Notorious space, it's quite
Obvious
To always be honest for an
Outstanding result,
Not knowing that you are
Yoked.

15. Harmony

Humility is among those that
Are together as one by being
Rational toward each other's
Most smallest needs
On a
Never ending courtship that last for
Years to come.

16. Godspeed

Giving all glory and honor to
Our most high
Does much good. Being in a
Sanguineous state is always
Positive,
Especially when you have given up on
Everything that has
Dominated your life.

17. Apposite

Apple of the eye is not as
Passionate as a grape, but is as
Pretty and colorful as an
Orange that is
Sweet as sugar from a cane that
Is taller than endless patience and
Tolerant while being
Easy going with each other.

FOUR

Eternal Love

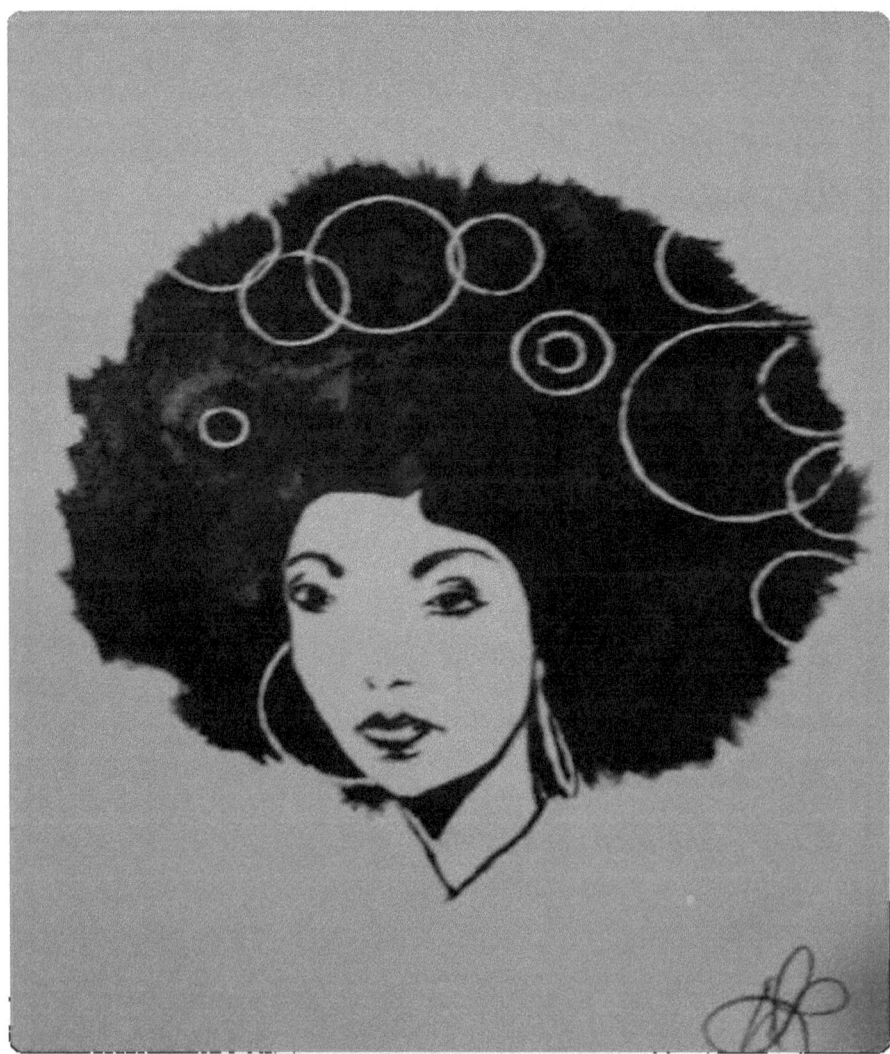

Chapter Three – Eternal Love

Eternal Love is a "veil being uplifted" from a dark shadow waiting to be revealed, yet lasting indefinitely.

Poem List:

1. Tie
2. Crush
3. Chat
4. Facetious
5. Listener
6. Network
7. Merge
8. Union
9. Link
10. Parity
11. Bliss
12. Cohesion
13. Friends

1. Tie

Together you are an
Increasingly an
Eloquent match.

2. Crush

Calmly you two should
Ravish the enchanting love
Until each is
Satisfied with a remarkable
Heartfelt feeling.

3. Chat

Communication is the key to a good partnership because
both parties
Help one
Another
Through any given situation.

4. Facetious

For those of you who never laugh or joke with each other, you will
Always be unhappy because being a little
Cartoonish is not bad at all. If you try to
Embrace in each other's arms
To spark an
Inevitable relationship that no one can
Oppose
Unequivocally due to your togetherness being
Set.

5. Listener

Learning to pay close attention to your lovers
Inner thoughts and feelings
Shows that you are a
Tender heart with an
Exuberant and
Nice conversation PEACE, being
Empathetic because he or she needs to
Release.

6. Network

Needing each other is the best
Entertainment that one can
Truthfully share
With open arms, and a loving feeling that's
Original in nature, while being
Receptive with an open mind and heart
Keeps the working bond anew.

7. Merge

Making all the moves from North, South,
East and West will
Refresh your loving relationship with lots of
Good humor toward an
Everlasting courtship.

8. Union

Uniquely you were joined together with
No intentions of ever departing
In spite of the
Opposition that you may face,
Nothing is going to stand in the way.

9. Link

Longevity will be yours forever as you display
Illustrious notoriety, for you should
Nevertheless continue your
Kindredship.

10. Parity

Putting each other's feelings first is set
Apart from not listening, while
Reassuring a comfort zone that's
Important and
Thoughtful for
You and your mate.

11. Bliss

Buying gifts on occasions is a
Lion heart, but what's most
Important is the
Sweetness of your
Sensational touch.

12. Cohesion

Carefully choosing friends and
Optimistically believing in your soul mate requires
Honesty which leads to
Everlasting
Security that
Impresses each
Other on every level of issues that
Needs mending.

13. Friends

Fervent hearts should always pray,
Relative to any geselskap,
Instead of annihilating a sincere rapport,
Established between individuals that
Need each other
Daily for
Support.

ABOUT THE AUTHOR

Dr. Rhemalyn Lewis-Williams, a poet, Executive Director/Founder, American Prince & Princess, Inc., mother of three, is a servant leader who supports many community and charitable causes.

Lewis-Williams attends Bibleway Church under the leadership of her husband, Pastor Samuel Williams, where she is the church treasurer, program director, and a praise team singer.

A native of Winstonville, Mississippi, who now lives in the capital city of Jackson, she holds a PhD in Social Work from Capella University and degrees from Jackson State University and Coahoma Community College.

Lewis-Williams is a member of the National Association of Social Workers, the National Association of Pageant Judges, Phi Alpha Honor Society of Social Work Majors, Zeta Phi Beta Sorority, Inc., and the Clinton Ink Slingers.

EVERLASTING *Love* Poems

written by **Dr. Rhemalyn Lewis-Williams**

cover illustrated by
Makeba Griffin

Your comments are welcome.
http://meredithetc.com/everlasting-love-poems/

Buy other Meredith Etc book titles

Meredith
a small press
Etc
Blog: meredithetc.com
facebook Meredith Etc
Meredith*etc*

The home of good books; **click, buy,** or **download** now! Visit: www.meredithetc.com